FULL THROTTLE:

"America's Obsession For More!"

by

Dennis Andrew Ball,

author, THE BALL DOCTRINE:

"Creating Peace & Prosperity In Every Nation!"

FULL THROTTLE: "America's Obsession For More!"

<u>DEDICATION</u>

"THIS BOOK IS DEDICATED TO AMERICANS

WHO SACRIFICE EVERYDAY TO PRESERVE

PROTECT & DEFEND OUR LIBERTY &

FREEDOM FOR OUR CHILDREN&

GENERATIONS TO COME!

NOW THE TIME HAS COME FOR A NEW

GENERATION OF AMERICANS TO TAKE THE

REIGNS OF STATE & MAKE THEM WORK AS

THEIR OWN IN THE BEST INTERSTS OF THE

PEOPLE, THEIR CHILDREN, THEIR FAMILIES

AND GENERATIONS TO COME!

TABLE OF CONTENTS

Dedication

Acknowledgment

Authors' Foreword

———

ACKNOWLEDGMENT

To The COURAGE Of The Mission To Show The World What They Are Required To Do To Know The Origins of Our Existence & How To Know It Personally.

Author's Foreword

I am reminded by history past the history of the United States would not be complete if it were not for those gallant men and women who in the face of danger, proceeded to do something Special about it! America's very existence is tied to her people THE PEOPLE since the founding by a Belief in a Supreme Being with an invisible hand guiding the United States of America.

Since the death of President Kennedy, events in America and the World have continued to show all of us how vulnerable our economic system is to currency manipulation and deficit spending by governments and the Congress of these United

States, the result being a bloated deficit with borrowing and spending unaccountable to The Citizenry & States of the United States; including fiscal policies, laws and acts contrary to The BEST INTERESTS of ALL Americans.

Author, Dennis Andrew Ball addresses these abuses showing the way out by generations of government entities have allowed to be created including every President since President Kennedy.

He also shows the history of America how through subterfuge and manipulation of her foreign & domestic policies put at risk our very ability to survive and thrive as a people & nation.

Read what must be done to bring America back to herself and her people in FULL THROTTLE: "America's Obsession For More!"

1. THE POLITICAL CLASS,

The *history of America* would not be complete if it were not for the men and women who sacrificed much of themselves for a new nation and their children. Of course, much can be said of those who plotted against them and used them to profit at their expense. For those they must answer for us we must correct their mistakes for our children and generations to come. This then, becomes the back ground for

FULL THROTTLE:

"America's Obsession For More!"

"You cannot help the poor by destroying the Rich." "You cannot keep out of trouble by spending more than you earn." "You cannot lift the wage earner by pulling down the wage payer" – Abraham Lincoln

---

"I have always been afraid of banks."

"One man with courage makes a majority" "It is to be regretted that the rich and powerful too often bend the acts of government to their own selfish purposes." "Take time to deliberate but when the time for action arrives, stop thinking and go in." – *Andrew Jackson*

Let it be said, that America's finest hours are yet to come because the Children Of America can make a contribution to not only our Nation but also the World!

We are the product of generations past, present and future with the belief that our rights come from God; NOT THE STATE at a great cost to those who fought and died for them! That was the Social Contract created in 1781 at Yorktown-Gloucester Bay, Virginia.

The monuments laid at the reefs of those so honored are a testament to the sacrifice of so many for the hope that their sacrifice would *bear.* A proud nation was born and with it the greatest nation on earth in the history of man, *"AMERICA!"*

THE NATIONAL BACKGROUND

Early History

What was assumed by those in power was taken for granted by those struggling to live out their dreams. *AMERICA* was a land of opportunity because it's people made it their priority to continue living out their dreams for a better life for themselves and those for their children.

Colonial America grew at an astounding rate by the span of time from the founding of the Republic at Jamestown, Virginia 1607 until the last entry known as Georgia Colony 1732.

Of course, many events in between the time of founding and establishing Colonial life dominated the culture legally and politically; particularly making it possible for 2.5 million people to realize their value because the Bible was read in the home, the schools and the Supreme Court! Ethics & Morales were also taught in the home practicing honesty and good business including honest services. The attitudes within the culture was fairness as the colonies grew in population and farming.

As a result, the *Great Migration* ensued so that by the beginning of the War For Independence, *AMERICA* had enough population to fight England for it. And so we did on July 4, 1776 by way of the Declaration Of Independence, Congress, Philadelphia, Pennsylvania.

Now comes "FULL THROTTLE:

"America's Obsession For More!"

Many of the colonists believed God blessed and reserved America for them to conquer and take dominion ownership of the land was contentious because Wars for land belonging to native populations were in dispute culminating in settlements agreed to by their Chiefs & Council Of Elders.

Fast forward to today's society, there still exists a system based representation of enumeration of census as to the number of folks that occupy individual states. However, the 16th Amendment did away with the census enumeration and went to a direct tax on income which now includes the Standard Deduction and deductions based on gains and losses. This is the problem America is plagued.

Could it be those with the most to lose tie themselves up with the government for as long necessary to keep themselves from being penalized for surreptitious acts they commit during the period of doing their business?

That is my point, unlike the history of *Early America* when life and government was much simpler and much smaller than now, we Americans did not have to deal with so much regulation & taxation without representation. Executive session was not the experience as it is *today, meaning less transparency.*

And So, since President William Howard Taft, a man who held Office as both President and later as Chief Justice, history records his participation in the events that mark 1913 as a Turning point in American history.

Events do have a way of marking themselves to follow the outcome of what creates tremendous conflicts and tragedy in the lives of our Citizens & our Children.

It is within this context that government *Of, By & For The People* will survive and thrive in this the twenty-first century and beyond because 'God IS Alive' in the nation and the World!

FULL THROTTLE is that vehicle to get us where we can understand what must get done to correct the problems created by our national loss of sovereignty that can restore our standing in the World and put an end to the mindless currency manipulations from European & Domestic Bankers.

They whom own the Gold controls the masses. *AMERICA* must take back her economic sovereignty by correcting the structural decay allowed to be created in order to make every other model obsolete in the process of governing our People and assisting generations to come.

Moses receives the 10 Commandments from

God on Mount Sinai. From there God shows

Himself to the Children of Israel by a Cloud

during the day and a pillar of fire by night.

God knew a visual was important for them

to see his evidence from the tabernacle.

2.ENTITLEMENT IS A DISEASE.

Now we turn to God & how he wants us to know Him to do what we are created to do.

The Bible speaks to the origins & creation of the World & Universe. Genesis 1

God revealed to Moses how the World began and the relationship he desires with his creation. This is the central theme of this title & brings into focus how we are to function. Fast forward to the Exodus from Egypt the Children Of Israel wandering in the Sinai 400 years after Joseph had become the Pharaoh's minister of finance [vizier] both to the Pharaoh & to the Egyptians.

Joseph's visions and interpretations came as gifts from God to show His power to the Pharaoh through his servant Joseph.

God heard the prayers of his people and decided to raise a leader in Moses to guide them out of Egypt to the promised land.

The Bible talks about all the conflicts that resulted but that God won and his people were freed from the slavery they suffered.

Is America suffering from years of emotional and financial abuse caused by greed and forces conspiring to destroy our nation and make us and our children slaves to the State?

Have we become a nation of indifference personal gain & profit by any means possible?

This is the core of the problems facing the Nations and the World, but that God has provided a better way for all of us to function in a Global way.

THE TABERNACLE

While in the Sinai desert, God spoke to Moses and the Children Of Israel to make Him a Tabernacle made of cloth and goats hair, Exodus 25:8.; 33:14-16.

He wanted to walk amongst His people. But what does this signify? For many of us

God is an amorphous being without a clearly defined shape or form.

The only hint of his appearance is how He appears before his servants in different ways absent a body but appearing as holiness.

What is the significance of a God who is Holy but desires to walk amongst His People? An important question to show us God's way.

2. THE [ISMS] HAVE IT..

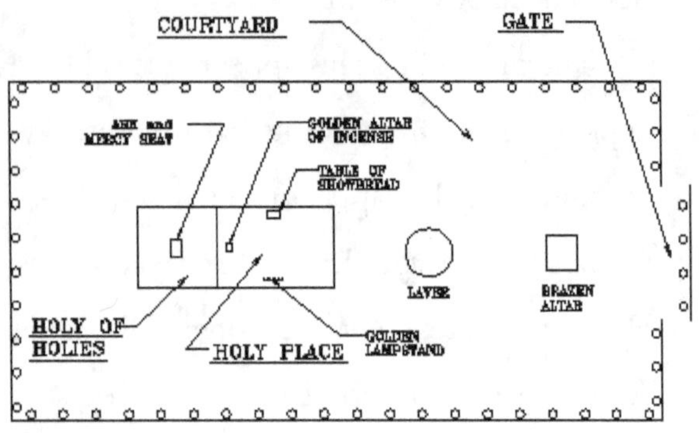

The Tabernacle served Obe purpose of
God showing His people that he was their

for them. So important. Moses was allowed to communicate in the presence of God himself in the Holy of Holies at the Mercy Seat.

It is my contention that the Mercy Seat Of God is available to all believers in the Triune God of Father, Son & Holy Spirit.

But unlike the physical appearance of an actual tabernacle in which God dwells, we are the tabernacle in body & soul that he dwells.

It is there that we can come to him in our mind and ask Him: "What Do You Want Me To Do?"

This is no different than what Moses did in the Holy Of Holies. Moses communicated with the Triune God giving us His laws known as the 10 Commandments.

People of FAITH have an opportunity to know God as he really is in your Spirit. He

will lead you to the Truth about Himself,
His Son and His Holy Spirit. *"Ask Him What He Wants You To Do?"* Then do it!

4. A NATION OF MISFITS.

"IT WAS SHOW TIME IN THE SINAI DESERT WHERE MOSES MET GOD"

EXODUS 19:1-25, 20:1-26

The Ten Commandments

I. I am the LORD your God:
you shall not have strange Gods before me.

II. You shall not take the name of the LORD
your God in vain.

III. Remember to keep holy the LORD'S Day

IV. Honor your father and your mother.

V. You shall not kill.

VI. You shall not commit adultery.

VII. You shall not steal.

VIII. You shall not bear false witness against
your neighbor.

IX. You shall not covet your neighbor's wife.

X. You shall not covet your neighbor's goods.

God made himself known as the Creator of the universe showing his plan for the nations by creating a "Special People" for them to walk with Him.

The power of prayer comes from a personal relationship with Father God. When Moses met God, he was not looking for Him. But God sought him because He heard the prayers of His people four hundred years after Joseph.

Father God made a covenant with the Hebrews when Abraham left his tribe to follow the voice of God. The history of the Jewish State can be traced back to what God told them to do in the Desert at the time of their emancipation from the clutches of Egypt.

This becomes the basis for the Nation Of Israel and for those who have lived to see & record her history.

5. GOOD V. EVIL!

Now the State of Israel is tested daily by Islamic Palestinian terrorists who rain down Rockets & grenades on their neighborhoods.

God said enmity would be the product of their division though they share in common Father Abraham. We are witnessing years of abuse produced by warring nations against the People Of God.

It is time to change the dynamic of the Paradigm engulfing this planet and to bring forth a new model by which nations adopt.

I have attempted to show that God is no respecter of person but Just & Equitable to His creation. We are made in His image by which we all share conscience. That's what makes us special in His economy.

The family is His creation from birth to

death.

It is shameful when there is an attitude of indifference that permeates society's norms. We are living in a parallel universe of fact & fiction affecting our lives.

Good versus Evil cloaked in secrecy impacting the outcomes of family unity creating conflicts that only can be solved by strong leadership with the community for it's Best Interests,

That means approaching problems with an emphasis to jump in and solve them.

Those who would conspire to destroy another are only creating their own fall. God is Sovereign and causes events to change the outcome of others. Our security ultimately depends on Him.

We create our own destiny by obeying

His Commandments. This is always the test of a Nation & their families &communities. Karma is real & visits all of us because the laws of nature are unforgiving.

The Sins of the Fathers are visited upon the children. But Father God has given us a way out if we will take it. What is that way?

We will explore it in Chapter 6, the WAR AGAINST DARKNESS.

6. THE WAR WITHIN.

What is the War Against Darkness?

What is the War Against Evil?

"And God said of the Tree you may freely eat in the garden except the tree in the middle you shall surely die." Genesis 2:16;3:3.

Hence the World has never recovered from disobedience by Adam & Eve. Disobedience to God's directives has continually caused great harm to His creation by which many lives have been lost both physically and emotionally.

God is not mocked Galatians 5:6-7. His creation is perfect but darkness inhabits it and causes great injury to those within it.

How was it that the Children Of Israel could survive in the Desert for forty years as a nomadic tribe of wanderers to form a nation after their own kind?

In spite of what God showed Moses about the Origins of life, where do you suppose he got his knowledge?

God spoke to him in the Tabernacle which the priests recorded in the Torah, the record according to God.

The Glory of God shown upon him and

he was transformed from ordinary to special for he had found favor with the Creator because He obeyed God. Very important. He did what God wanted of him and continued to serve God's people with authority.

Yet some who declared their loyalty opposed Moses. They were Jannes & Jambres, two magicians of the carnal arts. Antagonists without name also encamped themselves within the twelve tribes.

God used death to cleanse His people before they were allowed to enter the land promised to them by Abraham's covenant with God.

In the Book Of Numbers, the history of Israel shows that Korah the high priest in the Tabernacle led an insurgency against Moses divine authority.

Dathan & Aribram came along from Egypt Causing Moses lots of conflicts with his leadership questioning his authority given him by God.

The World is full of those who question God's authority in other people plus their own.

The New Jerusalem described in the Book Of Revelation coming down from Heaven reveals the future of God's creation On Earth, The Tabernacle of God.

It describes the World of the Lost in Hell and the World of the Righteous whose names are written in the Lambs Book Of Life.

Because He is a Triune God, we will never understand but what we are given to know. It is in this life for us to find and become that which He reveals about us and is expected.

Dathan   *&*   *Abiram*

Korah with son Izhar falling.

7. AMERICA'S OBSESSION.

Our destinies are tied to our walk with God. Allowing Him to direct our paths to righteousness when it is inconvenient.

Our hope is to enter His presence by our fervent prayers that availeth much. Listen to Him speak to you by His spirit like Moses in The Desert later in the Holy Of Holies in The Tabernacle of God.

The difference now is that your body is His tabernacle that dwells from within you. Use it to communicate as a semiconductor in the Holies. This is where He dwells. His Spirit lives within you but may be dormant because it has not been used as intended. To change it make it work for you. Come into the Holies in your mind like Moses found God at Sinai in the Burning Bush. Ask Him

"What Do You Want Me To Do?" Then listen to him ask Him questions have an interactive communication. This to me is know God.

If we are to be the "Salt" of the earth, it's our responsibility to know what to do. I'm not a church follower who follows, I Lead. God gives His gifts to those He can Trust. "Can He Trust You? Really?

If He asked you to Jump! Would you ask, "How High?" This is not some hypotheses put forth to substantiate one's relationship, but a realistic walk that produces results for you with the living God.

Faith is the key ingredient in knowing Him. When Moses met God, he had none. Moses faith grew as he interacted with Him. Interact with Him! He is waiting for you!

8. THE CRISIS WITHIN.

How did this change? Moses killed defending a slave woman from being raped by an Egyptian who attacked her.

He was reluctant to go back to Egypt not knowing how he would be received. Much fear possessed his mind but God gave him helpers through his extended family.

His brother and sister, Aaron & Miriam were there with him in Egypt as his family witnesses and support. They were with him after they left Egypt met God & roamed for forty years in the Desert to the Promised Land of Israel.

As I have said in other titles, "If your Not Working For Your Family, Whom Are Working fore?" This is a key principle of Life & Longevity. God created the family!

He included it in His Ten Commandments. "Honor your Father & Mother that you may Live a long and good life." God knew what he was doing to protect His people.

Unfortunately, many people do not know or seek what to do to resolve this conflict in their lives. Many don't even care what the consequences are regarding their conduct.

For that they have no one to blame for drug addicted life they live unfulfilled & depressed. The crisis within their souls is real and causes much anxiety as they traverse life without God and hope for a better future.

Some find themselves homeless and unable to cope with their life's condition. Some recognize they have options and pursue them with the support of others.

It is this author's opinion that each of us has an opportunity to discover our destiny by the works we engage. Karma is a real force of life that visits everyone when time and distance shrink.

The Bible speaks of it in several of the Old & New Testaments. There is moral law within *the natural laws* of God for all human behavior to acknowledge and follow; especially as it relates to the wellbeing of the family unit.

Our hope is to learn and grow in "faith" to bring others into the Kingdom of God for all humanity to acknowledge for the benefit of their children and generations to come. This is our ministry to shine the light for all to follow into the Kingdom of God to make a World safe for us and for our children.

The Kingdom Of God is neither a place nor a State of Mind but a Dimension that defies time & space.

Some have described It as being released from the mother's womb into a Universe unlike any other.

9. GETTING IT RIGHT.

From Moses to Jesus and all parties in between, God is faithful to His Word and what He intends for all of us.

But because of "Free Will", He allows His creation to choose for whom they will serve. This is the dilemma humanity falls into.

Evil prevails in the land and makes life difficult for honest people. This is the point of concern when one becomes United rather than Divided with their Heavenly Father.

Coming to the point of acknowledging Our need for our Heavenly Father becomes a huge turning point in our lives. Making contact with Him is too!

How you become in contact with Him is an act of your will and what you believe

He wants you to do. That is something God must show you after you ask Him.

God the Father, God the Son & God the Holy Spirit are three-in-one, a Trinity. No one understands it but Scripture affirms it

No one can realize it without personally experiencing it. That experience is coming to know Father God. How do we do it?

10. CHANGE FROM WITHIN.

From Heaven God Came Down To Faith!

The Triune God of the Universe decided to make Himself known to His creation in the flesh to show he cared for the billions of us who love Him.

This has always been the message for us to receive. God is a righteous force for our lives. Our lives depend on what happens to them by those closest to us.

The act of praying recognizes God the Father is listening & watching in His Seat. His Son Jesus is too. The Holy Spirit is the Intervener of His will and fulfills it.

Knowing God is to know Him perfectly. It means being born again not of the flesh but by the Spirit. When One comes to know God they come as children acknowledging their flaws and their sins. Moses had his, killing a soldier of Pharaoh's Court attempting to rape a Hebrew slave. Exodus 2:11-15.

To know God is to love God by His total Personage. We accept Him by faith and come before Him as children.

CHRIST DIED FOR OUR SINS

The transition between the tabernacle of God by Moses and the tabernacle of God's Son, Jesus Christ is one of personal will.

Are We prepared to acknowledge our need for a Savior who cared enough to die and rise to prove God's will for our lives?

Because we worship a Triune God, it is imperative we explore the depths of His being by acknowledging His presence in our lives. This is Remaking from Within.

Since are bodies are the Temples of

God, our lives are the Tabernacle of God & provides us to go to Him in our minds as if we are in the Holy of Holies in the Kingdom of God.

This is what God wants for us to know Him and to love Him. His love for us passes all understanding once we experience it for ourselves.

ASK HIM INTO OUR LIVES

Every generation has both the burden, responsibility & opportunity to know God. Born of a virgin, Mary mother of Jesus bore God's son traced from the lineage of Judah.

To know God in His totality is to know the power of His being and the forgiveness for our sins. The Cross where the nails were driven through his hands, the beatings He took on our behalf is witness of God's love for His creation and our humanity. His Resurrection and Ascension Holy Spirit Empowerment has given us to power our Lives in the Kingdom of God.

This is the Power Of God For YOU! & An end to America's Obsession For More At ANY COST!